You Be the Bread and I'll Be the Cheese

Showing How We Care

Titles in This Set

About the Cover Artist

Laura Cornell loves to illustrate children's books. Even
when she was little, she drew extra characters in her
storybooks! Now she lives with her young daughter in
New York City.

ISBN 0-673-80023-7

Copyright © 1993
Scott, Foresman and Company, Glenview, Illinois
All Rights Reserved.
Printed in the United States of America.

Acknowledgments appear on page 144.

2345678910 VHJ 99989796959493

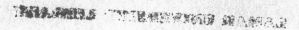

You Be the Bread and I'll Be the Cheese

Showing How We Care

ScottForesman

A Division of HarperCollins Publishers

Contents

Being Together
Genre Study

Helping Hands

Celebrations

MOLLY the BRAVE and ME

By Jane O'Connor
Illustrated by Sheila Hamanaka

Molly has guts. She has more guts than anybody in the second grade. She can stand at the top of the monkey bars on one foot. She doesn't mind it when Nicky hides dead water bugs in her desk. And if big kids pick on her, Molly tells them to get lost.

Molly is so brave. I wish I was like her.

Today on the lunch line Molly said to me, "Beth, can you come to our house in the country this weekend? It is lots of fun there."

Wow! I guess Molly really likes me. That made me feel good.

But I have never been away from home. What if I get homesick? What if they eat stuff I don't like? What if there are lots of wild animals? I was not sure I wanted to go.

I sat at a table with Molly. I said, "Gee, Molly. It sounds neat. Only I don't know if my parents will say yes."

That night Molly's mom called my mom. My mom said yes. So how could I say no?

It was all set. Molly's parents were going to pick me up on Saturday morning.

Friday night I packed my stuff. Later my mom tucked me in bed.

"I'm scared I'll miss you," I said. "I bet I'll cry all the time. Then Molly will think I'm a big baby. And she won't like me anymore."

My mom hugged me. "You will have fun. And Molly will understand if you are a little homesick."

Then my mom kissed me two times.

"One kiss is for tonight. The other is for tomorrow night when you will be at Molly's house."

Molly's parents came early the next
morning. I was scared, but I was excited, too.
Most of all I did not want to look like a wimp
around Molly. So I waved good-bye to my
parents and hopped in the back seat.

Molly's dog sat between us.

"This is Butch," said Molly. Right away
Butch started licking me. I'm kind of scared of
big dogs. But did I show it? No way! I acted like
I loved getting dog spit all over my face!

By noon we got to Molly's house. It sat all alone at the top of a hill.

"This was once a farm," Molly's mom told me. "It's 150 years old."

I like new houses. They haven't had time to get any ghosts. But I didn't say that to Molly's mom.

Right after lunch we went berry picking.
That sounded like fun. Then I saw all the beetles
on the bushes.

I did not want to touch them. But Molly just swatted them away. So I gave it a try too.

"Hey! This is fun," I said. "I have never picked food before."

We ate lots and lots of berries. Red juice
got all over my face and hands. I pretended it
was blood and I was a vampire. I chased Molly
all around.

"You know what?" I told her. "I am really
glad that I came to your house."

Later we went looking for wild flowers. That sounded nice and safe to me. We walked all the way down to a stream.

A big log lay across the stream. Molly ran right across it. Boy, what guts! Butch ran across too.

I stared at the log.

"Aren't there any wild flowers on this side?" I asked.

Molly shook her head. "The best ones are over here. Come on, Beth. Don't be scared. Just walk across—it's easy."

"Okay," I told myself. "Quit acting like a wimp."

I started taking tiny steps across the log. Near the end I slipped. Oof! Down I went.

"Are you all right?" Molly asked.

I nodded, but my backside really hurt.

We picked flowers for a while. And when we left, I crawled across the log. Molly didn't tease me. Still I knew I looked like a jerk.

On the way back to the house Butch saw a rabbit and chased it into a field of corn.

"Dumb dog!" said Molly. "He will never catch that rabbit. We'd better go and find him."

20

"Oh, rats!" I thought, but I went in after Molly. We followed the sound of Butch's barks.

Boy, was that field big! The corn was way over our heads, and it seemed to go on for miles.

At last we spotted Butch. Molly ran and hugged him. Then she pulled me by the arm.

"This place is creepy," Molly said. "Let's get out of here."

That was fine with me! But it was not so easy getting out. All the corn looked the same. It was hot and hard to see. Bugs kept flying in our faces. It felt like we were walking around and around in circles.

"Can't Butch help us find the way?" I asked.

Molly shook her head. "Butch can't find his own doghouse."

Then Molly started blinking hard. And her nose got all runny. "Beth," she said. "We're really stuck in here. I'm scared."

Molly scared? I could not believe it! I held her hand. "Don't be scared," I told her, even though I was scared too. "We'll get out of here."

Then I got an idea.

"Come on," I told Molly. I started to walk down the space between two rows of corn. I did not make any turns. I stayed in a straight line.

"Pretend this is a long street," I said. "Sooner or later we have to come to the end of it."

And at last we did! Molly and I hugged each other and jumped up and down.

Woof! Woof! went Butch.

"Hot stuff!" said Molly. "You got us out."

When we got back to Molly's house, her mother said, "Where have you girls been? It is almost time for dinner."

Molly told her parents about following Butch into the corn. Then she put her arm around me.

"I was scared stiff," Molly told them. "But Beth wasn't scared at all. Boy, does she have guts!"

Guts? Me? I couldn't believe my ears!

Dinner was great. We cooked hot dogs on sticks over a fire. And there was plenty of corn on the cob.

"Oh, no! Not corn!" Molly and I shouted together. But we each ate three ears anyway.

Right before bed I did get a little homesick. Molly's mom gave me a big hug. That helped.

Then Molly told me I was her best friend. We locked pinkies on it. That helped too.

Maybe Molly was right. Maybe I really am a kid with guts!

THINKING ABOUT IT

1. Beth and Molly are both brave, and they show it in different ways. How have you shown that you are brave?

2. What do you think about *Molly the Brave and Me* as a title for this story? Does it fit, or should it be called something else? Why do you think so?

3. What might happen if Molly and Beth go to an amusement park together? How might each girl feel about the rides and games? Why?

ANOTHER BOOK BY JANE O'CONNOR

In *Sir Small and the Dragonfly,* a dragonfly swoops over the town of Pee Wee and carries away Lady Teena. Who will be brave enough to rescue her?

The Summer My Relatives Came

by CYNTHIA RYLANT

Cynthia Rylant

I write best about true things. When I was six years old and living with my grandparents in Cool Ridge, West Virginia, this crazy group of relatives came up from Virginia one summer to visit us.

Uncle Earl helped Grandaddy fix things. Aunt Eunice curled Grandmama's hair. Aunt Agnes told stories while Aunt Wanda cooked pinto beans and cornbread for supper. Grandmama canned tomatoes. Roger and Peter chased cows. And the other relatives just kept on eating and sleeping and playing. The adults always included the children in all the family activities. That made us feel very important.

The time came for them to pack up and leave us. They said, "You all come see us now." We did, the very next summer.

And when I grew up, I wrote about us all in *The Relatives Came*. I sent copies to West Virginia and to Virginia, where the relatives still live. We had become famous!

The Relatives Came

Story by CYNTHIA RYLANT   Illustrated by STEPHEN GAMMELL

It was in the summer of the year when the relatives came
They came up from Virginia. They left when their grapes
were nearly purple enough to pick, but not quite.

They had an old station wagon that smelled like a real
car, and in it they put an ice chest full of soda pop and
some boxes of crackers and some bologna sandwiches, and
up they came—from Virginia.

They left at four in the morning when it was still dark,
before even the birds were awake.

They drove all day long and into the night, and while they traveled along they looked at the strange houses and different mountains and they thought about their almost purple grapes back home.

They thought about Virginia—but they thought about us, too. Waiting for them.

So they drank up all their pop and ate up all their
crackers and traveled up all those miles until finally they
pulled into our yard.

Then it was hugging time. Talk about hugging! Those relatives just passed us all around their car, pulling us against their wrinkled Virginia clothes, crying sometimes. They hugged us for hours.

Then it was into the house and so much laughing and shining faces and hugging in the doorways. You'd have to go through at least four different hugs to get from the kitchen to the front room. Those relatives!

And finally after a big supper two or three times around
until we all got a turn at the table, there was quiet talk and
we were in twos and threes through the house.

The relatives weren't particular about beds, which was good since there weren't any extras, so a few squeezed in with us and the rest slept on the floor, some with their arms thrown over the closest person, or some with an arm across one person and a leg across another.

It was different, going to sleep with all that new breathing in the house.

The relatives stayed for weeks and weeks.

They helped us tend the garden and they fixed any broken
things they could find.

They ate up all our strawberries and melons, then
promised we could eat up all their grapes and peaches
when we came to Virginia.

But none of us thought about Virginia much. We were so busy hugging and eating and breathing together.

   Finally, after a long time, the relatives loaded up their
ice chest and headed back to Virginia at four in the
morning. We stood there in our pajamas and waved them
off in the dark.

We watched the relatives disappear down the road, then we crawled back into our beds that felt too big and too quiet. We fell asleep.

And the relatives drove on, all day long and into the night, and while they traveled along they looked at the strange houses and different mountains and they thought about their dark purple grapes waiting at home in Virginia.

But they thought about us, too. Missing them. And they missed us.

And when they were finally home in Virginia, they crawled into their silent, soft beds and dreamed about the next summer.

Drawing The Relatives Came

by STEPHEN GAMMELL

Stephen Gammell

When I first read Cynthia Rylant's story, I thought of all my relatives and the big gatherings we used to have. Scenes from my childhood came to mind, like playing train in big boxes, or eating all over the house. I tried to draw scenes in such a way that when *you* look at the book, you may think, "Hey, I remember doing that," or "She kind of reminds me of my aunt," or "I had a blue truck like that!" Did you say things like that while reading the story?

I also thought it would be fun to put some of my own relatives in the drawings. My dad is cutting hair. Mom is standing and saying goodbye. Grandpa and Grandma are digging in the ground by a tree. And that's me playing the guitar. Can you find us? Maybe you'll notice one of *your* relatives or even see yourself!

50

The one thing that I always want when I draw is a sense of fun. Ever since I was a little kid, it was fun to draw. It still is! And I want that to come across in my illustrations. So when I'm choosing a story to illustrate, I look for funny situations. Then I wonder if I can add to them to make them funnier.

DAD →

MOM →

    I try not to change the story. For example, in *The Relatives Came*, many scenes I drew aren't actually described in the words, but they add something to the story. See if you can find some of them, and then think what *you* would draw. That's the great thing about picture books—they can get you to think about what *you* would do, how *you* might draw it, or what *you* would add. That's the fun of it!

Thinking About It

1. Find a picture in *The Relatives Came* that you would like to be a part of. Where will you be in the picture? How will you join the relatives?

2. Tell how *Molly the Brave and Me* and *The Relatives Came* could be about you or people you know. What happened in the stories that could happen to you? Tell why you think so.

3. All the relatives enjoyed their reunion! What do you suppose will happen next summer? Explain why.

Another Book by Cynthia Rylant

In *Henry and Mudge and the Bedtime Thumps*, Henry and his dog Mudge visit Grandma. Grandma has never met big, drooly Mudge before, and Henry is worried.

Helping Out

Words and photographs
by George Ancona

Helping out can be as simple as being there to hand someone a tool when he needs it.

In early spring, you can help to plant seeds in the vegetable garden. Soon they will sprout and grow into many good things to eat.

You can turn some chores into fun, like
washing the car on a hot summer's day.

You can spend a cozy winter afternoon
in grandpa's workshop helping to sort out
all those mixed-up nails, screws, nuts,
and bolts.

When you own a boat, you must scrape
the barnacles off the bottom before putting
it back in the salt water.

No matter where you live, the kitchen,
with its warm, good smells, is a great
place to help. Except for slicing an onion,
which makes you cry.

Feeding the baby can be a funny, yucky job.

Some jobs can be dirty, like changing the oil in the engine of a car.

When you work alongside an adult and do
a good job, you feel pretty big.

But the best thing about helping out is
that it can bring two people closer together.

When you work alongside an adult and do
a good job, you feel pretty big.

But the best thing about helping out is
that it can bring two people closer together.

Thinking About It

1. This article shows many ways that children help. Tell how you help. If this article had a photo of you helping out, what would the photo show?

2. Pick a photo in the article. Be the person who took the photo. Tell why you took that photo. Tell how it goes with the article.

3. When we help people, we show that we care. How can we help around school?

AMELIA BEDELIA HELPS OUT

by PEGGY PARISH

pictures by LYNN SWEAT

"Have a good day," said Mr. Rogers. "And you help your aunt, Effie Lou."

"I will," said Effie Lou.

"I'll come back for you late this afternoon," said Mr. Rogers. He drove off.

"What a grand house," said Effie Lou.

"Miss Emma is a grand woman," said Amelia Bedelia.

She went to the door and knocked.

"Come in," called Miss Emma.

Amelia Bedelia and Effie Lou went inside.

"I am glad to see you," said Miss Emma.
"Sumter is sick and my garden is a mess."

"Don't you fret," said Amelia Bedelia. "We
will take care of that. Just tell us what to do."

"First," said Miss Emma, "weed the garden."

"All right," said Amelia Bedelia. "Is there
anything else?"

"Yes," said Miss Emma. "But go ahead and
start before the sun gets hot."

"Come on, Effie Lou," said Amelia Bedelia.
"Let's get busy."

They went to the garden.

"It does have a lot of weeds," said Effie Lou. She started to pull one.

"Stop!" said Amelia Bedelia. "What are you doing?"

"Trying to get the weeds out of the garden," said Effie Lou.

"Get them out!" said Amelia Bedelia. "She said to weed the garden, not unweed it."

"Oh," said Effie Lou. "I wonder why she wants more weeds."

Amelia Bedelia thought.

"Those weeds are little," she said. "Maybe vegetables get hot just like people. They need

big weeds to shade them. That's why Miss
Emma told us to weed before the sun gets hot."

"That makes sense," said Effie Lou. "I see
some really big weeds."

"Let's get them," said Amelia Bedelia.

They did. Soon that garden was weeded.
Amelia Bedelia and Effie Lou went back to
the house.

"The garden is weeded," said Amelia Bedelia.

"Good," said Miss Emma. "Now I want you
to stake the beans. Here is the string to tie
them. You can use this saw to cut the stakes."

"All right," said Amelia Bedelia.

"There are bugs on the potato plants. Take this bug powder and dust them," said Miss Emma.

"If you say so," said Amelia Bedelia.

The telephone rang. Miss Emma went to answer it.

Amelia Bedelia found all the things she needed. She and Effie Lou went back to the garden.

"All right," said Amelia Bedelia. "We will steak the beans first."

"Have you ever done that?" said Effie Lou.

"No," said Amelia Bedelia. "But she just said to steak them. Anybody can do that."

"Can I help?" said Effie Lou.

"Yes," said Amelia Bedelia. "You count the bean plants."

Effie Lou counted and said, "There are fifteen."

Amelia Bedelia unwrapped a package. She shook her head and said, "That's a mighty little bit of steak for fifteen plants. But it was all she had."

She took the saw and cut the steak into fifteen pieces. "I could have cut better with a knife," she said.

"Why didn't you use one?" said Effie Lou.

"Didn't Miss Emma say to use this saw?" said Amelia Bedelia.

"Yes," said Effie Lou.

"Then that's why," said Amelia Bedelia. "Now hold the steak while I tie it."

Amelia Bedelia and Effie Lou steaked those beans. "All right, beans," said Amelia Bedelia. "Enjoy your steak."

Effie Lou laughed. "Your work is fun," she said.

"That it is," said Amelia Bedelia. "Now those bugs are waiting to be dusted."

"How do we do that?" said Effie Lou.

"I'll catch and you dust," said Amelia Bedelia. "Here bug, here buggy, buggy, bug."

They caught and dusted every bug.

"Why did she want us to do that?" said Effie Lou. "Most people want bugs killed."

"But Miss Emma is not most people," said Amelia Bedelia. "Those bugs may be her pets. They are pretty little things."

"If you like bugs," said Effie Lou.

"That takes care of that," said Amelia Bedelia. "Let's go in."

"I made lunch for you," called Miss Emma. "After you eat, throw some scraps to the chickens."

"All right," said Amelia Bedelia.

"And Amelia Bedelia," said Miss Emma, "my garden club is meeting here this afternoon. Please make a tea cake."

"I'll be glad to," said Amelia Bedelia. "I do love to bake."

Amelia Bedelia and Effie Lou ate their lunch.

"I wonder where she keeps her scraps?" said Amelia Bedelia. "I'll ask her."

She went to Miss Emma's room. She came right back.

"We will have to look for them," said Amelia
Bedelia. "She's asleep."
They looked and looked.
"Here's a whole bag of scraps," said
Effie Lou.
"Good," said Amelia Bedelia. "Take some
and we'll throw them to the chickens."

They went out to the chicken pen. Effie Lou threw the scraps. The chickens came running.

"Look at that!" said Amelia Bedelia. "I never knew chickens liked to play."

"Aren't they funny?" said Effie Lou.

"They sure are," said Amelia Bedelia. "But I've got to get that tea cake made."

"I never heard of tea cake," said Effie Lou.

"Neither have I," said Amelia Bedelia.

"Then how can you make one?" said Effie Lou.

"Well," said Amelia Bedelia, "I know what tea is and I know what cake is. I'll put them together and I'll have tea cake."

"That's easy," said Effie Lou.

Amelia Bedelia got a mixing bowl. She put a little of this and some of that into it. She mixed and she mixed.

"Now for the tea," she said. Amelia Bedelia opened some tea bags and mixed the tea into the batter.

"It looks awful," said Effie Lou.

"Different folks have different tastes," said Amelia Bedelia. She poured the batter into a pan. Soon that cake was baking.

Amelia Bedelia began to mix another cake.

"What kind are you making now?" said Effie Lou.

"Nut cake," said Amelia Bedelia. "Miss Emma loves that."

Finally the cakes were baked.

"Are you going to put icing on them?" said Effie Lou.

"That's a good idea," said Amelia Bedelia. "It will fancy them up." She mixed white icing and pink icing.

"You ice the tea cake pink," she said. "I'll ice the nut cake white."

They finished the cakes and put them away.

Miss Emma came into the kitchen.

"The cake is ready," said Amelia Bedelia.

"It smells good," said Miss Emma. "There's one more thing I want you to do. There is a bare spot in my front lawn. Please sow these grass seeds on it."

"We will be glad to," said Amelia Bedelia. "Come on, Effie Lou."

They went out front.

"That spot is bare," said Effie Lou.

"It sure is," said Amelia Bedelia. She sat down and took two needles and some thread from her bag. She threaded the needles.

"Here is yours," she said. "Now, let's sew."
Amelia Bedelia and Effie Lou sewed those
grass seeds on the bare spot.

"Tie the ends together," said Amelia Bedelia.
"We don't want the seed to fall off."

They went into the house. Miss Emma was
in the kitchen.

"Let's walk around some," she said. "Show
me what you've done."

"All right," said Amelia Bedelia.

They walked by the chicken pen.

"Land sakes!" said Miss Emma. "What are those colored things?"

"Scraps," said Amelia Bedelia. "Those chickens did have fun."

"My quilting pieces!" said Miss Emma. "My good quilting pieces!"

"Did we use the wrong scraps?" said Amelia Bedelia. "Go get them, Effie Lou."

Miss Emma walked to the garden. She stopped and stared. "Those weeds!" she said. "Those big weeds!"

"We got the biggest we could find," said Amelia Bedelia.

Miss Emma looked at Amelia Bedelia.
"Thank goodness Sumter will be back soon,"
she said. "Why didn't you stake the beans?"

"We did!" said Amelia Bedelia. "There just wasn't much steak to give them. Show her, Effie Lou."

Effie Lou held up a bush.

"There goes my dinner," said Miss Emma.

She looked at the potatoes.

"I see the bugs are dead," she said.

"Dead!" said Amelia Bedelia. "Did we dust them too much? I'll get you some more."

Miss Emma laughed and said, "I can live without them. You've done enough."

"We enjoyed doing it," said Amelia Bedelia.

"I've seen all I want to see," said Miss Emma.

They all went inside.

"The ladies should be here soon," said Miss Emma. "The table is set. The tea is made. You can put the cake on this tray."

"All right," said Amelia Bedelia.

"I'll let the ladies in," said Miss Emma. She left the kitchen.

"Let's get the cakes ready," said Amelia Bedelia. "I hear the ladies coming now."

Soon Miss Emma called, "Amelia Bedelia, please bring the tea."

"Coming," said Amelia Bedelia. "Bring the cakes, Effie Lou." Amelia Bedelia set the tea tray in front of Miss Emma.

"Go ahead and pass the cake," said Miss Emma.

Every lady took some cake.

"I'm starved," said Mrs. Lee. "I can't wait for the tea." She bit into her cake.

"Delicious!" she said. "I've never tasted this kind before."

"You've never tasted nut cake?" said Miss Mary.

"This isn't nut cake," said Mrs. Lee.
"Try the pink kind."

"It is good," said Grandma Wilson.
"Hand me another piece."

"There," said Miss Emma, "your tea is
poured."

"Who cares about tea?" said Mrs. Mark. "I
want more pink cake."

"Emma, do tell us what kind of cake this is,"
said Mrs. Bloom.

Miss Emma took some cake.

"My favorite," she said. "Nut cake."

"No, the pink kind," said Ella Jean. "Try the pink kind."

But all of the pink cake was gone.

"Stop keeping secrets," said Grandma Wilson. "What kind of cake was that?"

"Ask Amelia Bedelia," said Miss Emma. "She made it."

A car horn honked outside.

"Mr. Rogers!" said Amelia Bedelia. "Come on, Effie Lou."

Miss Emma followed Amelia Bedelia to the kitchen.

"What kind of cake was the pink one?" she asked.

Amelia Bedelia looked puzzled.

"Tea cake," she said. "That's what you said to make."

"Tea! You mean—" said Miss Emma. She began to laugh.

Amelia Bedelia saw something.

"Oh, I plumb forgot," she said. "Your grass seeds."

Miss Emma looked at them. She laughed harder and put them around her neck.

"Amelia Bedelia," she said, "you are really something. Effie Lou, you are lucky to have Amelia Bedelia for an aunt."

"I know," said Effie Lou. "Amelia Bedelia knows everything."

The horn honked again.

"Hurry, Effie Lou," said Amelia Bedelia. "We can't keep Mr. Rogers waiting."

Thinking About It

1. Amelia Bedelia always gets mixed up! Sometimes words confuse her. What words have mixed you up? Tell what happened.

2. "I've seen all I want to see," said Miss Emma. What had she seen? How do you think she felt when she said it?

3. Think of a way Amelia Bedelia could help out someone you know. What do you think might happen?

Another Book About Amelia Bedelia
In *Amelia Bedelia Goes Camping*, Amelia Bedelia tries to *hit the road* and *row a boat*. What do you think she does?

The Mother's Day Sandwich

STORY BY
Jillian Wynot

PICTURES BY
Maxie Chambliss

"**G**et up, Hackett," said Ivy. "It's Mother's Day. We have to make a surprise for Mama."

"Prize?" said Hackett.

"Yes," said Ivy. "We're making her breakfast in bed."

Hackett followed Ivy into the kitchen.

"Hmm," said Ivy. "What should we make?"

"Cake?" said Hackett.

"No, silly," said Ivy. "We're not allowed to use the oven."

"Egg?" said Hackett.

"No," said Ivy. "I can't turn
the eggbeater and hold the
bowl at the same time.

It would dance all around
and fall off the counter
and smash.

Besides, we would still need
the stove."

Hackett opened the refrigerator. "Fruit?"

92

Ivy looked at the honeydew. "We'd need a sharp knife," she said.

Hackett took out a jar of mayonnaise.

Ivy frowned. "Put that back, Hackett," she said. "No one eats mayonnaise plain."

Hackett took out the pickles.

"*Yuck!*" said Ivy.

Hackett took out a stick of butter.

"You are being silly," said Ivy.

Hackett giggled.

"I know," said Ivy. "We'll make cornflakes with milk and a banana. Mama can cut the banana herself. And orange juice."

Hackett smiled.

Ivy climbed up on the counter and opened the cabinet. "Hmm. Maybe the cornflakes are in the back." Out came tuna fish, crackers, coffee and beans, soup, pears, raisins and noodles, jelly, spaghetti, vinegar, tomato sauce, tea, cookies and sardines.

"There they are!" Ivy took down the tall box and poured.

"Oops," she said. "I'll clean those up later."

The milk was too high for Hackett to reach.
He dragged a chair to the refrigerator and
climbed up. He set the container on the chair
and climbed down.

Plop!

"Oh, Hackett!" Ivy sighed. "We'll mop that up
later. But maybe I should get the orange juice.
You get the banana."

The bananas were stuck together at one end. Hackett tugged and pulled and squeezed, but he couldn't get one loose. He picked up the whole bunch of bananas and thumped them on the table.

"Hackett, *no!*" yelled Ivy. "They'll be all smushed and mushy."

Hackett started to cry.

"Don't cry," said Ivy. "I think there's one that's still good. I'll get the banana. You get the spoon and the knife."

At last everything was neatly arranged on the tray.

"Ready, Hackett?" asked Ivy.

"Wait," said Hackett. He ran out to the yard. He ran back in with a bunch of yellow buttercups.

"Perfect!" Ivy arranged them in a little pink vase in the center of the tray. Then she held her finger to her lips. "Shh," she said. "Let's be as

quiet as mice. We want Mama to be surprised."

They tiptoed to Mama's room.

Mama was fast asleep. Silent as fog, they tiptoed in.

Slowly, Ivy lowered the tray.

Quietly, Hackett unfolded the tray's feet.

Carefully, slowly, quietly, they set the tray down around Mama.

"Now?" whispered Hackett.

"Now!" whispered Ivy.

"Happy Mother's Day!" they shouted.

"Wggfcch! *Ughff! Hunh?*" Mama sat up with a jerk. The tray toppled over. Orange juice and milk, cornflakes and smushed banana, buttercups and water went flying.

"Oh, my," said Mama. "What's all this?"

Ivy and Hackett started to cry.

"It was supposed to be a surprise," said Ivy. "For Mother's Day."

Mama wiped banana off her nose. "Well, you certainly surprised me," she said, laughing.

Ivy smiled.

Hackett giggled.

"Come here, you two," Mama said. "Do you know what I would really like? A Mother's Day sandwich."

"A sandwich for breakfast?" asked Ivy. "I'll make it."

"No, me!" said Hackett.

Mama pulled them back. "You don't make a Mother's Day sandwich in the kitchen. You can make it right here."

"Here?" said Ivy.

"Yes," said Mama. "You be one slice of bread, Ivy. And Hackett, you be the other slice. And I will be the cheese."

Hackett and Ivy giggled.

"Now, listen, you two pieces of bread," said Mama. "Squeeze very close to the cheese, so it can't fall out."

Ivy and Hackett squeezed very close to the cheese.

"Happy Mother's Day," said the two slices of bread.

"Thank you," said the cheese.

Thinking About It

1. "Wggfcch! Ughff! Hunh?" Ivy and Hackett's mother was surprised! Describe surprises or gifts you have given to your family. Explain how the surprises turned out.

2. Milk, cornflakes, bananas, and buttercups— all over the bed! Which pictures help tell how Mama felt? Be Mama. Tell how you felt about your surprise and what you did about it.

3. If Ivy and Hackett planned a Father's Day surprise, what would it be? Why do you think so?

Brother

by Mary Ann Hoberman

I had a little brother
And I brought him to my mother
And I said I want another
Little brother for a change.

But she said don't be a bother
So I took him to my father
And I said this little bother
Of a brother's very strange.

But he said one little brother
Is exactly like another
And every little brother
Misbehaves a bit he said.

So I took the little bother
From my mother and my father
And I put the little bother
Of a brother back to bed.

Fito

Chito

Tito

Lalito

The Four Brothers

by Charlotte Pomerantz
pictures by David Díaz

Fito is a farmer and he lives in Aguadilla.
Chito is a teacher and he lives in Guayanilla.
Tito is a poet and he lives in a tree.
But Lalito is a baby and he lives with me.

Fito married Fita and they had a son Fitito.
Chito married Chita and they had a son Chitito.
Tito still writes poetry and lives in a tree.
But Lalito is a little boy and lives with me.

When Fitito grew up, he got married to Fitita.
When Chitito grew up, he got married to Chitita.
When Tito got old, he came down from the tree.
And Lalito, my Lalito, no longer lives with me.

Now Lalito is a plumber and he lives in Aibonito,
With Lalita, who's an engineer and works in Naranjito,
And they have a little son, very little, muy chiquito,
And they named him—did you guess it?—Willy.

CHARACTERS

A Father (or Mother)

A Boy (or Girl)

THINGS YOU WILL NEED

A book   A chair

A picture of a snake

A picture of a gorilla

A picture of a seal

Come Quick!

A PLAY FOR APRIL FOOL'S DAY
by Sue Alexander

The father is sitting in a chair in his living room. He is reading the book. The boy comes running in.

BOY Father! Come quick! There's a gorilla in my room!

The father looks up from his book.

FATHER Don't be silly. That's an April Fool's joke. Of course there is no gorilla in your room!

He reads his book again.

BOY But, Father, the gorilla is jumping up and down—like this!

The boy jumps up and down and scratches himself as a gorilla would.

FATHER I must say, you make a very good gorilla! But now I want to read my book. Go into your room and find something to do.

The boy goes out slowly. He runs back in.

BOY   Father! Now there's a snake in my room, too! He is wriggling around and saying HSSSSSS!

The father puts down his book and stands up.

FATHER   That's enough! First you tell me that there is a gorilla in your room! That he is jumping around like this!

He jumps around like a gorilla.

Now you tell me there is a snake in your room! And he is saying HSSSS! Those are just silly stories! And I want to read my book. Go to your room!

The boy goes out slowly. The father sits down and reads his book again. The boy runs back in.

BOY   Father! PLEASE come quick! Now there is a seal in my room! And he is saying GWARK! And he is clapping his fins together—like this!

The boy bounces like a seal and claps his hands.

GWARK! GWARK!

113

FATHER Hmmm. Maybe I had better go and look after all. If those animals ARE in your room, we will have to call the zoo!

He puts down his book and gets up and goes out.

BOY Ha! Ha! I did it! I made him look! And there's nothing there! What a good April Fool's joke!

The father runs back in, very excited.

FATHER You were right! There IS a seal in your room! And a snake! And a gorilla! AND THEY ARE ALL ON YOUR BED! We had better call the zoo!

The boy jumps up. He is very surprised at what his father has said.

BOY WHAT? How can that be? I'd better go see!

He runs out. He comes back carrying the pictures of the seal, snake and gorilla. He is smiling.

FATHER And a happy April Fool's Day to you, too!

They laugh and go off together.

Thinking About It

1. What trick have you played on someone? What trick has someone played on you? Who had more fun?

2. Show how you will make this play fun to hear and see. Which parts will people like best? Tell why.

3. HSSSSSS! Gwark! Gwark! The author made up noises and actions for the animals in the play. What animals could you add to the play? What noises would they make? What would they do?

MORE PLAYS BY SUE ALEXANDER

Come quick! There are six more plays for you to perform in *Small Plays for Special Days* by Sue Alexander.

Hello, Amigos!

By **Tricia Brown**
Photographs by **Fran Ortiz**

Hello, amigos! My name is Frankie Valdez. I live in the Mission District in San Francisco with my mother, my father, my three brothers, and my four sisters.

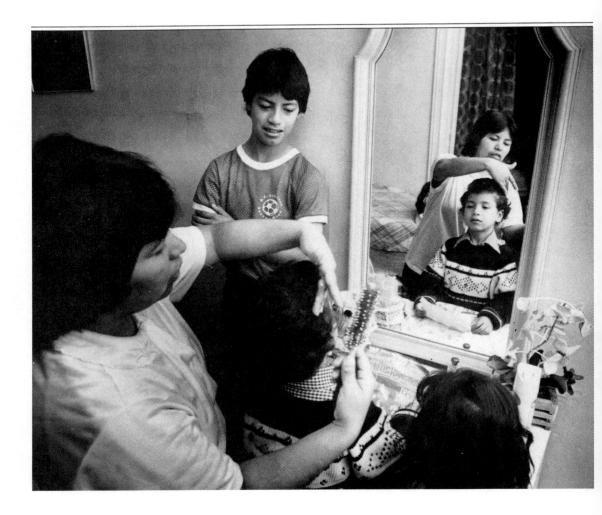

Today is my birthday. As my mother helps me get ready for school, my brother Gabriel wishes me a Feliz Cumpleaños—that means "Happy Birthday" in Spanish.

I feel so happy today. When I get home from school we will have my birthday party.

My sister Nancy and I go to the same school. The bus ride takes a long time. I like to look out the window as we drive through the city.

I always sit with my best friend, Marvin Martinez. Marvin hurt his arm. At school I help him fix his sling. Maybe I'll be a doctor when I grow up.

There's the school bell. It's time for breakfast.
Mmmmmmm . . . this leche is good.

At my school the first and second graders are in the same
classroom. Some of us speak Spanish at home, and we learn
English here at school.

Our first lesson is math. Sometimes I don't get it.
Mrs. Giddings, my teacher, helps me to understand. She
speaks Spanish, too.

Next we have recess. I love to play outside!

After recess we study English. I like English best when I get the right answer.

During science Mrs. Giddings shows a movie about mammals. My sister likes it, but it makes me sleepy.

During P.E. we play kickball. Because it's my birthday,
Mrs. Giddings lets me serve first. After P.E. everyone
surprises me with a birthday cake and a corona to wear.

I like to eat lunch with my friends, but today I eat quickly
and clean up early.

At my school we go
home after lunch.
I can't wait to get
home and have my
birthday fiesta.

Yippee! I'm finally home.

My mom says it will be a few hours before the party starts.
She wants to make some guacamole and sends me to the
market for some avocados.

When I get back I want to go to the Columbia Park Boy's
Club. My mom says that before I go, I need to finish my
homework. Luckily, my older brother, Gabriel, and my older
sister, Claudia, help me.

Then Gabriel and I walk to the Boy's Club.

Frank, the program director, is teaching me how to play pool. After my lesson I try to wait for Gabriel and his friend, Tyrone, to finish their game of foosball.

When we get home it's almost time for my party! I change into my party clothes and put on the corona my teacher made for me. I watch my mother mash the avocados with her molcajate.

Hmmm . . . delicioso!

My mother and father invite our family, friends, and neighbors to eat our favorite Mexican food—enchiladas, frijoles refritos, arroz, tortillas, and, of course, the delicious guacamole.

Chava, my father's friend, stops by to sing some songs on his way to work. He is a mariachi and sings in a nearby restaurant.

My favorite food is my birthday cake!

After we eat I get to break the piñata. When the piñata breaks, everyone gets to pick up the candy.

It has been a wonderful day. Papa and I walk to our church. He helps me light a candle, and I count my blessings.

Pulling It All Together

1. Now it's *your* turn. If Fran Ortiz took pictures of you on *your* birthday, what would they be? Why?

2. Mmmmm! Good! Who would you like to make a surprise meal for you—Amelia Bedelia, Ivy and Hackett, or Frankie Valdez's mom? Explain your choice.

3. Everyone in this book is getting together for the Fourth of July. You're invited too. Plan the activities for the day. Decide which character will be in charge of each one. Explain your choices.

Another Book About Birthdays

Learn all about birthday celebrations and the traditions behind them in *Happy Birthday!* by Gail Gibbons.

Books to Enjoy

Arthur's Great Big Valentine
Written and illustrated by Lillian Hoban
Since Arthur's best friend isn't speaking to
him, Arthur is not looking forward to
Valentine's Day.

A Special Trade
by Sally Wittman
When her elderly friend becomes ill, young
Nelly remembers the fun they had when he
used to push her in a stroller.

Jam Day
by Barbara Joosse
Illustrations by Emily Arnold McCully
A yearly family reunion of berry picking and
jam making reminds Ben how large his family
really is.

Jimmy's Boa and the Big Splash Birthday Bash

by Trinka Hakes Noble

Illustrations by Steven Kellogg

Jimmy's birthday party at SeaLand turns into a soggy mess after Jimmy's mom is kissed by a whale!

Our Home Is the Sea

by Riki Levinson

Illustrations by Dennis Luzak

A young Chinese boy lives on a boat and dreams of becoming a fisherman like his father and his grandfather.

Grandma's Baseball

Written and illustrated by Gavin Curtis

When a young boy's grandmother comes to live with his family, she always seems to be grumpy. But one day, the boy discovers Grandma's special talent.

Tonight Is Carnaval

by Arthur Dorros

It's time for Carnaval! A young Peruvian boy is excited because he will play in his father's band for the first time.

Literary Terms

Characters

Characters are the people or animals in a story. You can learn about characters from what they do and say. What do you learn about Amelia Bedelia from what she says and does?

Humorous Fiction

Funny stories that come from an author's imagination are called **humorous fiction.** *Amelia Bedelia Helps Out* is humorous fiction.

Mood

Mood is the way a story makes you feel. Pictures can help you understand the mood of a story. How do you feel when you look at the pictures in *The Relatives Came?*

Photo Essay

A **photo essay** is a group of photographs that tell about something. The photographs often have words that explain them. Frankie Valdez tells about his birthday in the photo essay *Hello, Amigos!*

Realistic Fiction

A story that could really happen is **realistic fiction.** *The Mother's Day Sandwich* is realistic fiction. Just like Ivy and Hackett, many children try to surprise their mothers on Mother's Day.

Setting

The **setting** is *where* and *when* a story takes place. *The Relatives Came* takes place in the country during the summer.

Glossary

Words from your stories

allow to let someone do something; permit: *My parents allowed me to stay up late.* **allowed, allowing.**

amigo SPANISH. a friend: *Elena and Willie are* amigos. *amigos.*

arrange to put in some kind of order: *The books were arranged in alphabetical order.* **arranged, arranging.**

avocado a tropical fruit shaped like a pear and colored green and black: *Cut up an avocado to put in the salad.* **avocados.**

barnacle

barnacle a small saltwater animal with a shell: *Barnacles attach themselves to rocks, docks, and the bottoms of boats.* **barnacles.**

beetle

beetle an insect. Its front wings cover its back wings when it is not flying: *The ladybug is my favorite beetle.* **beetles.**

blessing anything that makes one happy and contented: *Carlos thinks his pets are his greatest blessings.* **blessings.**

blink to open and shut the eyes quickly: *The bright light made her blink.* **blinked, blinking.**

brave without fear: *The brave girl pulled her little brother away from the burning garage.* **braver, bravest.**

cabinet   a piece of furniture with shelves or drawers: *A dining room cabinet holds dishes.* **cabinets.**

chore   a small or easy job that one does regularly: *My chore is setting the table.* **chores.**

container   a box, can, jar, or anything that can contain or hold something: *Dad keeps his nails in different containers.* **containers.**

containers

counter   a long table or shelf where work is done. Food can be prepared and eaten at a counter: *Stack the dishes on the counter.* **counters.**

country   1. land outside a city: *There were many farms in the country.* 2. the land and a group of people with the same leaders. *Our country is the United States.* **countries.**

country

dust   1. fine, dry dirt: *The wind covered the porch with dust.* 2. to get dust off; brush or wipe dust from: *We dusted all the furniture.* 3. to sprinkle with powder: *The mother dusts her baby with powder after its bath.* **dusted, dusting.**

dust

engine

engine   a machine that does work or makes something move: *Many engines are run by gas or electricity.* **engines.**

extra   more than what is usual, expected, or needed: *There is one extra desk in this classroom.* **extras.**

fret   to be cross or worried: *Don't fret if you can't go with us.* **fretted, fretting.**

guacamole

gorilla   a large, hairy animal with long arms and no tail: *A gorilla is the biggest and strongest of the apes.* **gorillas.**

guacamole   a thick sauce made from mashed avocado: *Let's make some guacamole dip to go with the chips.*

hug

homesick   feeling sad or ill because one is away from home: *The children were homesick on their first night at camp.*

hug   **1.** to put your arms around something or someone and hold tight: *The little boy hugged his teddy bear.* **2.** a tight squeeze with the arms: *I like a hug when I am sad.* **hugged, hugging; hugs.**

lesson   something that you learn; something that you are taught: *We had a spelling lesson today.* **lessons.**

oil a liquid that comes from the earth: *Gasoline is made from oil.*

particular hard to please: *He is very particular about the books he reads.*

pretend to make believe something is real when it is not: *Let's pretend we're camping.* **pretended, pretending.**

quilt 1. a soft covering for a bed. *This quilt is pretty and it keeps me warm at night.* 2. to make a quilt: *Here are some scraps of material to use in your quilting.* **quilts; quilted, quilting.**

quilt

recess a short time during which classroom work stops: *We'll finish the game at recess tomorrow.* **recesses.**

relative a person who belongs to the same family as another, such as a mother, sister, or uncle: *My cousin is my favorite relative.* **relatives.**

scrap a small piece; a small part left over: *We put scraps of paper in the basket.* **scraps.**

scrape to rub off with something sharp or rough: *We scraped the peeling paint off the house.* **scraped, scraping.**

scrape

sew

sow

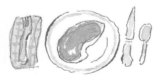

steak

seal a sea animal with thick fur: *Seals usually live in cold places.* **seals.**

sew to push a needle and thread through cloth. You can sew by hand or with a machine: *I sew all my own clothes.* **sewed, sewing.**

sling a loop of cloth worn around the neck to hold up a hurt arm: *He has his arm in a sling.* **slings.**

snake a long, thin animal with dry, rough skin and no legs. Snakes move by sliding along the ground: *A small green snake lives in our garden.* **snakes.**

sow to scatter seed on the ground; plant seed: *Dad sowed grass seed on some bare spots in the lawn.* **sowed, sowing.**

stake **1.** a pointed bar of wood or metal driven into the ground: *He tied the dog's leash to the stake.* **2.** to fasten with or to a stake: *We staked down the tent to keep it from blowing away.* **stakes; staked, staking.**

steak a slice of meat, especially beef: *They had steak for dinner.* **steaks.**

supper a meal eaten in the evening: *We had pizza for supper.* **suppers.**

swat to hit sharply: *I swatted the bug off my arm.* **swatted, swatting.**

tea cake a small cake to be eaten with afternoon tea: *Grandma made tea cakes for the party.* **tea cakes.**

tiptoe to walk on the tips of the toes: *She tiptoed quietly along the hall.* **tiptoed, tiptoeing.**

tiptoe

topple to tip; fall over: *The baby took two steps and toppled over.* **toppled, toppling.**

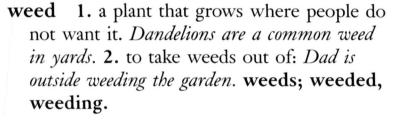

weed 1. a plant that grows where people do not want it. *Dandelions are a common weed in yards.* 2. to take weeds out of: *Dad is outside weeding the garden.* **weeds; weeded, weeding.**

weed

workshop a shop or building where work is done: *Mom has a workshop in the basement.* **workshops.**

wriggle to twist and turn; to move by twisting and turning: *The snake wriggled through the grass.* **wriggled, wriggling.**

Acknowledgments

Text

Cover: The title *You Be the Bread and I'll Be the Cheese* is drawn from the book *The Mother's Day Sandwich* by Jillian Wynot, pictures by Maxie Chambliss. Used by permission of Orchard Books, New York.

Page 6: *Molly the Brave and Me* by Jane O'Connor, illustrated by Sheila Hamanaka. Text copyright © 1990 by Jane O'Connor. Illustrations copyright © 1990 by Sheila Hamanaka. Reprinted by permission of Random House, Inc.

Page 30: "The Summer My Relatives Came," by Cynthia Rylant. Copyright © by Cynthia Rylant, 1991.

Page 32: *The Relatives Came* by Cynthia Rylant, illustrated by Stephen Gammell. Copyright © 1985 by Cynthia Rylant. Illustrations copyright © 1985 by Stephen Gammell. Reprinted by permission of Bradbury Press, An Affiliate of Macmillan, Inc.

Page 50: "Drawing *The Relatives Came*," by Stephen Gammell. Copyright © by Stephen Gammell, 1991. Illustrations from *The Relatives Came* by Cynthia Rylant, illustrated by Stephen Gammell. Illustrations copyright © 1985 by Stephen Gammell. Reprinted by permission of Bradbury Press, An Affiliate of Macmillan, Inc.

Page 54: From *Helping Out* by George Ancona. Copyright © 1985 by George Ancona. Reprinted by permission of Clarion Books, a Houghton Mifflin Company imprint.

Page 66: *Amelia Bedelia Helps Out* by Margaret Parish, illustrated by Lynn Sweat. Text copyright © 1979 by Margaret Parish. Illustrations copyright © 1979 by Lynn Sweat. Published by Greenwillow Books, a Division of William Morrow & Company, Inc. Reprinted by permission of William Morrow and Company, Inc. Publishers.

Page 90: *The Mother's Day Sandwich*, story by Jillian Wynot, pictures by Maxie Chambliss. Text copyright © 1990 by Jillian Wynot. Illustrations copyright © 1990 by Maxie Chambliss. All rights reserved. Reprinted by permission of Orchard Books, New York.

Page 106: "Brother" from *Hello and Good-by* by Mary Ann Hoberman. Copyright © 1959, renewed 1987 by Mary Ann Hoberman. Reprinted by permission of Gina Maccoby Literary Agency.

Page 108: "The Four Brothers" (text only) from *The Tamarindo Puppy and Other Poems* by Charlotte Pomerantz. Text copyright © 1980 by Charlotte Pomerantz. Published by Greenwillow Books, a Division of William Morrow & Company, Inc. Reprinted by permission of William Morrow and Company, Inc. Publishers.

Page 110: "Come Quick!: A Play for April Fool's Day" from *Small Plays for Special Days* by Sue Alexander. Text copyright © 1977 by Sue Alexander. Reprinted by permission of Clarion Books, a Houghton Mifflin Co.

Page 116: *Hello, Amigos!* by Tricia Brown, photographs by Fran Ortiz. Copyright © 1986 by Tricia Brown and Fran Ortiz. Reprinted by permission of Henry Holt and Company, Inc.

Page 136: Illustration from *Amelia Bedelia Helps Out* by Margaret Parish, illustrated by Lynn Sweat. Illustrations copyright © 1979 by Lynn Sweat. Published by Greenwillow Books, a Division of William Morrow & Company, Inc. Reprinted by permission of William Morrow and Company, Inc. Publishers.

Page 137: Illustration from *The Mother's Day Sandwich*, story by Jillian Wynot, pictures by Maxie Chambliss. Illustrations copyright © 1990 by Maxie Chambliss. All rights reserved. Reprinted by permission of Orchard Books, New York.

Artists

Illustrations owned and copyrighted by the illustrator.
Laura Cornell, cover, 1–5, 133–143
Sheila Hamanaka, 6–29
Stephen Gammell, 32–53
Lynn Sweat, 66–89, 136
Maxie Chambliss, 90–105, 137
Brian Karas, 106–107
David Díaz, 108–109
Roni Shepherd, 110–115

Photographs

Unless otherwise acknowledged, all photographs are the property of Scott Foresman.
Page 31: Courtesy of Cynthia Rylant
Page 51: Courtesy of Stephen Gammell
Pages 54–65: Photos by George Ancona
Pages 116–132: Photos by Fran Ortiz

Glossary

The contents of this glossary have been adapted from *My Second Picture Dictionary*, Copyright © 1990 Scott, Foresman and Company and *Beginning Dictionary*, Copyright © 1988 Scott, Foresman and Company.